CITY OF MARVELS

J. R. Carpenter is an artist, writer, and researcher working across performance, print, and digital media. Questions of place, displacement, migration, and climate change have long pervaded her work. Her digital poem, *The Gathering Cloud,* won the New Media Writing Prize 2016. Her debut poetry collection, *An Ocean of Static,* was highly commended for the Forward Prizes 2018. Her second collection *This is a Picture of Wind,* was listed in The Guardian's best poetry books of 2020 and longlisted for the Laurel Prize 2021. She is currently a Research Fellow working on *Wind as Model, Media, and Experience* at Winchester School of Art.
https://luckysoap.com

Also by J. R. Carpenter

Words for Worlds Upended	(Guillemot Press, 2020)
This is a Picture of Wind	(Longbarrow Press, 2020)
A General History of the Air	(above/ground press, 2020)
An Ocean of Static	(Penned in the Margins, 2018)
The Gathering Cloud	(Uniformbooks, 2017)
GENERATION[S]	(Traumawein, 2010)
Words the Dog Knows	(Conundrum Press, 2008)

Contents

ISBN: 978-1-915760-51-7

Cover designed by Aaron Kent

Edited and Typeset by Aaron Kent

Broken Sleep Books Ltd
Rhydwen
Talgarreg
Ceredigion
SA44 4HB

Broken Sleep Books Ltd
Fair View
St Georges Road
Cornwall
PL26 7YH

City of Marvels

J. R. Carpenter

Broken Sleep Books

York is a City of Marvels.

for Anthony Capildeo

I

a visitation. commencing.
with late gently. delayed.

the arrival. of pocket texts.
hastens. the anticipation.

of Anthony. of the lost hour.
in the apse. of the station.

II

at the edge. of a swathe. of shallow water.
overhung. by a sweep. of weeping willow.

a sign appears. heralding.
birds. of the campus lake.

followed. in quick succession.
by the apparition. of said birds.

having nothing. with which.
to make. an offering.

I stand. dumbstruck.
and gaze. upon them.

the Moorhen. stalks off. dowdy body.
teetering. on extravagant feet.

the mallard. expresses an enthusiasm.
disproportionate. to the situation.

of geese. there are Greylag.
Lesser Snow. and Canada.

what's good for the Gadwall.
is good for the Goosander.

of the Black Swan. no sign.
of the Mute Swan. no comment.

III

upon entering. a building.
upon entering. a room.

vapours. of white spirit.
rising. enveloping.

developing. an eye.
for a cupboard. of colours.

an affection. for a face. of type.
a feeling. for letter forms. ligaments.

fumbling. towards an understanding.
of blue. as an expectation. a thirst.

for the always. already sky.
of colonial. imagination.

squatting. to examine. drawers. of plates.
of religious themes. pastoral scenes.

objects. of advertisement.
bordering. on decoration.

a silver. of squiggles.
a thesis. of rivers.

a press. printing.
on thin ice.

IV

and in the morning.
the sky. a blue. defying.

southern expectations.
of a grey. north.

always.
already raining.

V

York. is a city. of towers.
half real. half imagined.

the scaffolding. of mannequins.
necks. of magnificent proportions.

of monsters. and marbled papers.
murals. of sharks. in the shambles.

maps. from other centuries. say.
you are here. you are here. you are.

watching. two women. sitting.
on a bench. wearing. tall. green.

plush. hats. fashioned.
in the shape. of pine trees.

adorned. with festive. decoration.
deep. in conversation.

VI

of other marvels. of a more pedestrian. variety.
York presents me. with a box. of willow charcoal.

anti-fog wipes. for glasses.
resulting. in the restoration.

of vision. a cure.
for blindness.

books. reflected. in the glass. of a framed print.
spines. spires. spines. spires. spines. spires.

a sycamore spreads. its arms wide. as the nave.
of York Minster. from this angle. at least.

the Minster has its own rose.
the rose has its own sun.

VII

bloody Romans. coming over here.
founding our cities. building our sewers.

leaving. broken columns. from the great hall.
of the fortress. of the sixth legion.

fallen. in the first century.
resurrected. in the twentieth.

it's upside down, a man insists.
his wife. and I. ignore him.

take a picture of me. with Constantine.
another man. demands. of his wife.

standing. next to a statue. of Constantine.
proclaimed emperor. in York. in 306.

an imposing figure. even seated.
in toga. and sandals. in this wind.

VIII

there's nothing standing.
between York. and Siberia.

my neighbour proclaims.
when I get home.

#ConeyStreetLife

(a history of right now)

...and now, and now, and now. how do we reside. in this relentless. ever-present. unfolding. minute by minute. walk slowly. note fleeting sights, sounds, smells, sunny spells, and snippets. of overheard conversations. everything is of interest.

where does a street start? within sight of it? out the back of it? under the river part of it? when does the water end? with flood floating the rowing club? blue edging the memorial gardens? that's a bit close, a woman says. and turns. to go.

people gather. to gander. at high water. look, someone left a bicycle! locked up, down there. a river walk? I don't think so, not today. if that's a road under there normally. jeepers. the river's right up. not where it was. not as high as last time though.

the wind bitter. a helicopter over. the city cruises. boats double parked. we would have gone on a boat. if it hadn't been high water. a mother explains. to a child. that would have been a lovely thing. to have done. to have. and to have not.

flood waters retreat. leave high and dry beaches. of silt. skirted. by pedestrians. by what gauge. a river then? barging over banks. sliding under bars. a bar is a gate. a gate. is a street. is a river a garment then? of light. rustling. under steel girders.

what's in a name? a crease on a map. a mark in a ledger. the king's street. a narrow lane. full of busy shops. difficult to know. it used to be that entrance. even narrower alleyways. leading off. to squares. and courts behind. we'll come back, I promise you.

an artery. has its capillaries. an alleyway. has its ventricles. air vents and bricked-up windows. what once passed. through these past portals. barrels. rolled off barges. into dank interiors. these short-circuits. between river and street.

walls. of a myriad. of materials. bricks. of different makes. colliding with medieval blocks. of limestone. tunnels. of sky and shadows. connecting past with present. solid with liquid. a couple turns a corner. can we cross here? not unless you want to swim.

the street turns. its back to the river. sinks. its stone teeth. deep. into ancient bank. raises. brick defences. concrete. against current. and still. the river rises. races. leaves silt traces. seeps.

look. there's a doorway. from the river. a tree. from a crack. in a wall furred. with green weeds. the ghost. of a bicycle. haunts silty shallows. a beach. under the Ouse Bridge. it's actually two bridges built side by side, a voice from the river cruise says.

the Ouse used to be wider. the sun used to be higher. the sky used its best blue. by twilight. gave the rest away. pausing. to watch the sculls slicing. bodies bent double. remind us. we weren't meant. to walk upright.

walking. under a dove-grey sky. reading. the street. through the soles. of blue suede shoes. stopping. to examine. a spray-painted X. in pale orange. marking a spot. where the pavement has cracked. a corner cut. in need. of attention.

tourist tat. in the windows. round the corner. yes, carry on, straight down. past the English bulldog. cast in silver plastic. shot glasses. flat caps. union jacks. and magnets of the Minster. and then the girl goes: I'm sorry, we don't take cash. oh my days.

yes, carry on. straight down. let's go have a look, see what there is. to let. new lower prices. brightening concealers. white trousers. already? all inquiries. is it warming up out there? it's chilly down here. in a sing-song voice: yes it is, yes it is.

cold! a cold wind. over and over. again and again. break the cycle. rewrite the story. oh look, sun! that guy...? a child asks. and swift comes an affirmation. as if part. of an ongoing conversation: he's not a ghost, he's real.

utopia. applicants must be flexible. this is what straight people said to us. discover beauty. that's what I said. boundless beauty. I said that. well say it again. top to toe radiance. do you know, that is lovely.

buy and sell. we fix. broken. on spot. no fee. time is of the essence. I live 2 miles away. so, York. yeah. stay and shop. your love stories. in the heart of the city. I don't actually know my way around, if I'm honest. well at least you've seen the scale of it.

a common lane. leading. into the city. along the edge. of a Roman fortress. formerly. a ward boundary. also dividing parishes. the boundaries of which. now run. through these premises.

a bomb. that keeps falling. creates an absence. lets sky in. what even is time? a great window. removed, for safekeeping. a gold leaf, gleaming. a sign warning: keep pigeons out. and peace within.

daffodils storm the city walls. no dogs allowed. no loading. a modern take. click and collect. trying to trick me. to force me. to put things. in my basket. I'm not sure, I says. I'll bring me own work, I says. we'll carry on tomorrow.

sky clouded. with blossom. a crowd walking. between the city walls. and the station. past the cholera burial ground. without stopping. to read the stones. sacred to the memory of. who departed this life. this one, this one, this one. it's here, in front of us.

a convoy. of wheelie cases. a hollow sound. of hard plastic. rolling over cobblestone pavements. past the ghost. of the Black Swan. early-18th-century journeys to London took four days. I've got like the flattest shoes on. I'm just like here for the ride.

centuries. of windows. of all shapes. and sizes. bricked over. to avoid taxes. light shut out. epidemic rife within. we have learned nothing. about ventilation. sorry to confirm. we're currently closed. probably went bust. sorry mum. sorry I called.

sitting. in a shop window. on a shopping street. as characterised by shops. shoppers. a pedestrian zone. a sweep. of polka dots. skirts past. a stream of feet.

red coat. orange coat. orange skirt. teal coat. fuchsia coat. burgundy hoodie with white zipper. pink plastic carrier bag. black leather handbag. wooden cane. metal cane with plastic handle. orange bike. high vis. vest. SECURITY. and then oddly empty for a moment.

aim a camera at a corner of the street. no feet come to it. remove the camera. the street is thick with feet. painful ankles in sandals. bare ankles in trainers. a long stride amidst amblers. a red bike. a green cane. heels and wide-leg trousers. a toddler. another. a limp.

modern shoppers at Next. like their countless predecessors at Leak and Thorp's. and those before them. who lodged at the famous George Inn. are as close as anyone can now be. to the geographical centre. of Medieval York Jewry.

what's original? a bit of brick wall. hardwood floorboards. some tile. what's next? past the bedding and lighting. bolsters and bulbs. eyelet curtains and bins with soft close lids. beyond the fuchsia stilettos. a curve. of rear window. a glimpse. of green river.

a quarter to twelve. all the bells ringing. all the street voices. chiming in. I come whenever the bus comes. I still have the house I grew up in. oh, here we are. oh wow, I don't know how to describe it. you don't want to go down that way. no no, I'm just thinking.

a street. bending slightly. in a cool breeze. is made. of air. and water also. misty. muggy. making us sleepy. milky. white cloud brightening. white gull screaming. white plane passing. silent. because distant. another plane. louder. because close.

what defines a street? a series of buildings. form straight lines. double yellow lines. subjects of alignment. zones of contact. between roadways and pedestrians. cobbles and pavements. gutters and rain. round the corner here. that's what I look at for fun, anyway.

Acknowledgements

In late autumn 2021, Anthony Capildeo, Writer in Residence and Professor at the University of York, invited me to print a short text at Thin Ice Press and to read with them in the evening. The next day, as I wandered aimlessly, it dawned on me, that York is a city of marvels.

From February-May 2022, I returned to York as Writer in Residence on StreeLife, an interdisciplinary research project exploring the history of Coney Street. My contribution was a history of right now. These short texts were initially written in a notebook as I walked the street, looking and listening. They were quickly edited as Instagram captions and posted to @ConeyStreetLife. I later letterpress printed 32 of these texts, in a limited edition of 55.

Thanks to Anthony Capildeo, JT Welsh, Helen Smith, Lizzy Holling, Nick Gill, and everyone involved with Thin Ice Press and StreetLife York. Thanks to Susie in Leeds and Justin & Dav in York for additional ground support. And special thanks to Heather Collins for table-sourcing, proofreading, and being a great friend during the period of this writing.

LAY OUT YOUR UNREST

Milton Keynes UK
Ingram Content Group UK Ltd.
UKHW040618171123
432742UK00004B/93

9 781915 760517